CARS

by Anne Rockwell

PUFFIN BOOKS

PUFFIN BOOKS
Published by the Penguin Group
Penguin Putnam Books for Young Readers,
345 Hudson Street, New York, New York 10014, U.S.A.
Penguin Books Ltd, 27 Wrights Lane, London W8 5TZ, England
Penguin Books Australia Ltd, Ringwood, Victoria, Australia
Penguin Books Canada Ltd, 10 Alcorn Avenue, Toronto, Ontario, Canada M4V 3B2
Penguin Books (N.Z.) Ltd, 182-190 Wairau Road, Auckland 10, New Zealand
Penguin Books Ltd, Registered Offices: Harmondsworth, Middlesex, England

Unicorn is a registered trademark of Dutton Children's Books.

Library of Congress number 83-14080
ISBN 0-14-054741-X

Published in the United States by Dutton Children's Books,
a division of Penguin Books USA Inc.
375 Hudson Street, New York, New York 10014

Editor: Ann Durell   Designer: Isabel Warren-Lynch

Printed in Hong Kong by South China Printing Co.

First Unicorn Edition 1986   COBE
10

Cars go everywhere.

They go on six-lane turnpikes

and on dusty, country roads.

They go through dark tunnels

and over airy bridges.

They go fast.

They go slow.

Gasoline makes them go.

There are big cars

and small cars,

old cars

and new cars.

Cars take us far away

and down the street to the store.

Our car is red and shiny.

We get in our car,

and away we go!